Published by Jastin Enterprises, LLC

Stock Imagery supplied by iStock, Storyblocks and Adobe

Any website addresses used in this book are fictitious, however, due to the changing nature of the Internet the web address characteristics may change since publication.

ISBN-13: **978-0692958308**

ISBN-10: **0692958304**

Dedication

BUILDING CYBER-READY WORKERS FROM A YOUNG AGE TO MEET NATIONAL WORKFORCE DEMANDS OF THE FUTURE

This book is dedicated to supporting the workforce needs for the 21st century in the areas of cybersecurity. Some surveys estimate that there were over 200,000 cybersecurity jobs left unfilled in 2015 and the demand will grow exponentially over the next 20 years. This book, and subsequent episodes, will educate and inspire a new generation of potential cyber technologists, workers and managers who will have had the opportunity to experience the cybersecurity territory from early childhood, thus making "cyber speak" and careers in this area much less foreign.

The book targets children between the ages of 8 and 12, as well as adults who like to read with them. Everyone can benefit from reading these episodes, in order to become safer online.

McGarry (2013) reported that General Keith Alexander, former Director, NSA, described cybersecurity work as a "tremendous opportunity" for young people…" He said; "This generation is coming up cyber savvy," after explaining how his almost 2-year-old granddaughter knows how to use an iPad to watch movies on Netflix. "We can train them. We can educate them."

Source: McGarry, B. (Oct. 14, 2013). NSA Chief: What Cyberwarrior Shortage?

ACKNOWLEDGMENTS

To all of my friends, family, colleagues and supporters of this effort, I thank you dearly.

~ and ~

To Roy, who fully supported all of my ideas with kindness, respect and endless love.

Jastin is twelve years old and is a very active

child on the Internet. In the last episodes about Phishing, Ransomware, Cyber Bullying, the Internet of Things (IoT), and Privacy and Identity Theft...

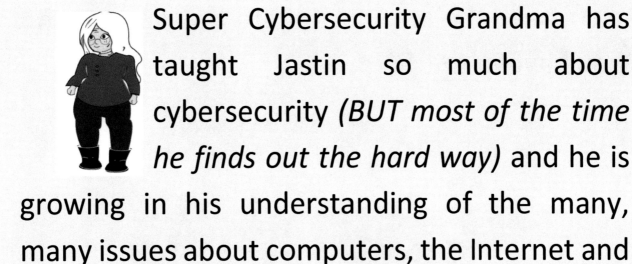 Super Cybersecurity Grandma has taught Jastin so much about cybersecurity *(BUT most of the time he finds out the hard way)* and he is growing in his understanding of the many, many issues about computers, the Internet and being safe in the digital world.

Jastin talks so much about his newly found cybersecurity knowledge and activities that his school decided to ask Super Cybersecurity Grandma to host a CYBER CAREER DAY (in celebration of the ***October National Cybersecurity Awareness Month***), for parents to come to the school to share the kind of jobs they have in this field.

This was a special day in that the parents didn't present the usual careers; Super Cybersecurity Grandma asked that they come and talk about the **"jobs of the future."**

Jastin's class was so amazed at how most of

the parent's jobs have something to do with cybersecurity and they didn't even know it.

Sam's father was the first one to "show and tell" about his job and how <u>NOW</u> cybersecurity is important to him.

He works at a big bank downtown. At first all he had to do was meet people at the bank window as a Bank Teller, take their identification cards and handle their bank business.

But now that "sooooo" many people never come into the bank, use ATM machines and do online banking his job has changed.

He has to care about "identity theft" which *Super Cee Gee* taught Jastin in a previous episode. He also added that bank account numbers are being stolen online and how hackers can take money  from someone's bank account without ever meeting them or coming to a physical bank.

His new job is called a **SECURITY ANALYST** where he stays on top of all of the activities that the Bad Guys participate in (viruses, hacking, etc.) and he makes sure everyone's money is safe.

He went to college to study banking and then he took extra training courses at work to learn about how cybersecurity changed the way banks work today.

Isaiah's mother was the next one to speak to the class. She has been a Police Officer for many years.

But now she is a **DIGITAL FORENSICS ANALYST** for the police department. Her job changed because criminals are using mobile phones, computers and the internet so much now, they leave a trail of information on the devices that helps the police officers solve the crimes in a brand new way.

Digital Forensics Analysts can find all kinds of information on the computer's hardware and software like the disk drive, memory and especially in cell phone texts, e-mails, social media, web sites visited, and other things that we use in the digital world. Isaiah's Mom didn't have to go to college to be a Police Officer, but later on she learned Digital Forensics by taking courses at a community college.

Tamika's mother is a cool television News Reporter. She is on television everyday talking about current events in politics that have to do with foreign countries hacking into the election systems in the United States, and other cyber-related world events that seem to happen on a daily basis.

She had to go back to school to study hackers, e-mail servers, data breaches, and other cyber stuff to help her know what she is reporting on.

She is now the **CHIEF CYBERSECURITY REPORTER**. She went to college to learn

Journalism to be on TV and had to also take cybersecurity courses after she graduated.

Of course, there are people like Gregory's dad who are real computer geeks! He has a cybersecurity job that lets him work on

networks, routers, computers, Wi-Fi and servers. He is actually one of those people who are close to the computers and knows what "**bits and bytes**" are going across the network to see what should and should not be there. He is called a **SECURITY ENGINEER**.

Gregory's dad actually works closely with Susan's dad who is also kind of *"geeky"*. He is what is called a **PENETRATION TESTER** or **"Ethical Hacker"** for the U.S. government.

Their jobs are cool because they get a chance to "legally" hack into computer systems so that they can tell people where a **black hat hacker** can get into their systems and steal data BEFORE IT HAPPENS!

The parent who has the most fun is Alice's uncle who gets to play what seems like computer games. It's called war gaming (because it started to be used in the military) or "red team / blue team" challenges. His job title is also **Penetration Tester**, but he likes to call himself a **"GAMER"**.

How does it work? The **red** team members are the **ATTACKERS** and use their skills to do bad activities (steal data, crash the network, etc.) to the blue team's network. The **blue** team members are the **DEFENDERS** and have to do everything they can possibly do to protect their network from the attackers. It's just like playing chess. Who wins? Whoever can protect their information the best. It's a great computer game type of job (that you can get paid for).

All three of these last parents studied computers and networks for a long time in school. They went to colleges and training centers to learn more about computers.

Jastin's brother was so impressed with the Gamer presenters that he decided to build his own gaming desktop. He bought all of the parts needed and had a great time putting them

together to make a "screaming" gaming PC. He didn't realize that in doing this he was taking the first step toward the career of becoming a **COMPUTER TECHNICIAN.**

The next presenter was Jennifer's aunt who writes computer code for "apps" and is called a **SOFTWARE DEVELOPMENT ANALYST.** She writes the actual programming code to make computers do what they are supposed to do. She also writes secure apps for mobile phones. Her job has become even more important because of cybersecurity so now she is called a **SECURE SOFTWARE DEVELOPER.**

She has to make sure that all of the programs that are created for computers, mobile phones, and the internet are safe from hackers. It's a hard job because there are so many hacks these days. She learned coding at a young age attending summer camps that taught children  how to code in "Python" and other computer languages.

One thing that the students didn't know was something called a **Security Clearance**. Because …… if you work for the United States

Government like some of the parents, you have to have one of these clearances. In order to get the jobs that they have, the government did a background check on everything in their lives to be sure they were "good citizens" and could be trusted with the government's information.

All of the parents and friends who talked about their jobs at Career Day passed the security clearance, but they know many people who didn't and could not get one of the good paying jobs.

Those people had bad credit, criminal records and even little bits of information online that they posted (that was not good). They didn't know that everything you do online can help or hurt you when you try to get a cybersecurity job that needs a security clearance.

Even the stuff you post on Facebook, Snapchat, Twitter and all social media places can come back and "bite you." Remember *Super Cee Gee* introduced Jastin to **"personal**

reputation" in a prior episode?

The last speaker was Javier's mother who is called a **CHIEF INFORMATION SECURITY OFFICER (CISO).** She has the **highest paying** job of everyone because she is usually the one who all of these cybersecurity professionals report to.

A CISO ("SIS-OH" -- that's how it is pronounced) has a lot of responsibility for making sure everyone and everything is secure in the company where they work. CISO's have people working for them like we mentioned earlier, Security Analyst, Secure Software

Developers and more. To be a CISO, she had to work hard, get a college degree and get experience working on cybersecurity stuff like networks, programming software, and network security.

She also took a very hard test and got what is called a "Certification" from an organization that verifies that a person knows something about cybersecurity. Education, experience and the certification helped her get her top ($$$$) job.

By the end of the day the class had so much information about cybersecurity jobs that their heads were spinning.

At least, now *Super Cee Gee* and the school were happy that the students knew something about the types of good-paying careers that are available to them (outside of the sports and entertainment industries) that they probably never heard of.

The jobs all are high paying and there are many openings for them in different companies and in the government. It gave the students some career choices to think about for the future!

Glossary

Bits and Bytes – Bits and Bytes are somewhat complicated terms but the easiest way to describe them is to say that they are how your information is passed along on computers, wires and computer networks. When you learn more about computers and communications you will see data is sent in 0s and 1s along the network which is the "language" that computers understand. The real computer "geeks" like studying this level of computer concepts. For many cybersecurity-related jobs, you don't need to know this level of detail.

Cyber Bullying – This term is often used to describe many undesirable activities and behaviors related to the Internet, social media, e-mail and texting. The term is derived from traditional bullying in schools, where children were threatened and mistreated in various ways. With so much use of the Internet now, the bullying activities take on a different form but the negative influences and actions are similar and more pervasive. As such, it has become very difficult to monitor and curtail. Everyone must be aware of this phenomenon so that cyber bully victims can be protected and cyber bullies can be taught to respect others.

Hackers and being Hacked – There are many kinds of hackers, good ones and bad ones. In the past episodes of Super Cee Gee, the focus has been on the hackers who are trying to get into computers, networks, and systems for bad reasons. Hackers can be one person working out of their home or a number of people in other countries working for large governments. "Black Hat" Hackers use their technology to break into someone else's computer, mostly to steal their information (like credit card information and passwords) to sell to others who buy the information illegally. We've learned about some of the ways (phishing and ransomware) that hackers use to get information for disreputable reasons.

Identity Theft – Identity theft happens when a hacker (or anyone else) has enough information about you like name, address, social security number, date of birth, school, parents' names, etc. in order to open bogus accounts in your name. Usually they create bank accounts, order credit cards and other accounts that will give them the opportunity to get money – money in your name that YOU may have to pay back. Even if you don't have to pay it back, Identity Theft can ruin your personal reputation. 1-800-IDTHEFT is the number to call for help!

Internet of Things (IoT) - In order to understand IoT, you need to know that computers communicate through the use of "addresses." Every internet device has to have this address to be located by another computer. This "Internet Protocol" (IP) addressing scheme is kind of complicated and you can learn more about that later. Today, there are many, many Internet addresses that we can associate with cars, refrigerators, alarm systems, mobile devices, light bulbs, thermostats and other things. Since these "things" can now communicate over the Internet – this term - IoT was coined. IoT is a good thing, and we easily buy and install devices because of the conveniences they provide - but with so many devices talking to each other and possibly sharing personal information, we need to think about some of the cybersecurity dangers.

Internet Privacy – Maintaining your privacy when you are online is a difficult thing to manage. Many people, young and old, freely put personal information in their social media accounts and give it online to companies from which we buy things. Also, as outlined in the Super Cee Gee "IoT" episode, some information is automatically collected by the devices we use. Online users have to be vigilant about protecting their personally identifiable information (PII) all the time.

Personal Reputation – Your personal reputation is what you carry with you throughout your life. In the digital world, it includes all of the information that exists on the Internet about you: pictures, friends, clubs, school, etc. It includes things that you posted and things that someone else has posted about you. It is important that you only have good things associated with your name and it starts with protecting your privacy and your online personality. As you get older, schools, colleges, and employers will be able to look at your online personal reputation.

Phishing – As a reminder from Jastin's first episode, Phishing attacks are named that because they are just like real fishing where someone throws out the bait on a fishing pole to catch a poor, unsuspecting fish and the fish bites the bait and gets reeled in? Well in the digital world hackers often send a bogus email to someone (the bait) hoping that some poor "schmuck" will think it's real and send their precious personal information to them. **Wrong**!

Ransomware – Bad software or (malware) that can stop people from accessing their pc, laptop, tablet or smart phone in essence putting a lock on files, pictures, data, contacts, and screens until a ransom is paid to the hacker.

Made in the USA
Middletown, DE
21 August 2024

59571104R00018